**To know Jesus is to love Him!
He is simply irresistible!**

To Charles-Edward, Israel, and Faith

Text Copyright © 2025 by Nancy Owusu Adu
Illustrations Copyright © 2025 by Christina Rudenko

Verses marked WEB are taken from the World English Bible.
All rights reserved. No part of this work may be reproduced or transmitted in any form or by any means, electronic ormechanical including, photocopying, or by any information storage or retrieval system, except as is explicitly permitted by the Copyright Act or in writing from the author.

ISBN: 979-8-9922853-2-1 - Paperback
ISBN: 979-8-9922853-3-8 - Hardcover

NBeirene Press

Who is Jesus to me?

By Nancy Owusu Adu

Illustrated by Christina Rudenko

My Closest Friend

Near and dear to my heart!
He knows me inside out
and loves me just the same!

He is a friend that sticks closer than a brother.

Proverbs 18:24

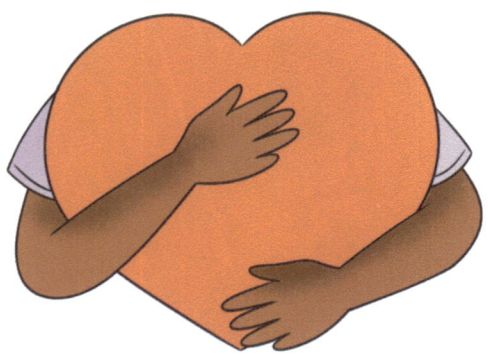

My Righteous Judge

His Highness!
Always fair, never partial.
Everything He says and does is right
I can trust His judgements.

He will judge the whole earth
with righteousness and fairness.

Psalm 98:9

My Good Shepherd

I don't worry about anything!
He cares for me and keeps me safe- far away from danger

I am the Good Shepherd. The Good Shephered lays down His life for the sheep.

John 10:11 WEB

My Amazing Guide

Go left! Turn right!
He shows me the way to go.
With Jesus as my guide,
I don't worry about making a wrong turn!

He guides me in the paths of righteousness
for his name's sake.

Psalm 23:3 WEB

My Strong Deliverer

Safe now!
He pulls me out of harm's way and hides me from evil. I will not be afraid of the devil's tricks

The Lord is my rock, my strength,
and my deliverer.

2 Samuel 22:2

The Great Healer

He heals me when I'm sick,
In no time I'm up and about! I am strong as can be, from my head right down to my toes!

He sends his word and heals me.

Psalm 107:20

My Great Comforter

When I'm sad and down, His words comfort me
Just like that, my heart is filled
with joy again!

Your rod and staff give me comfort.

Psalm 23:4

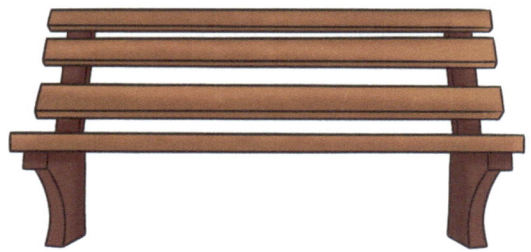

My Best Teacher

He teaches me all of life's best lessons.
With Jesus as my teacher,
I am sure to be the best I can be!

I will instruct you and teach you in the way
which you shall go. I will counsel you
with my eye on you

Psalm 32:8 WEB

My Powerful King

Ruler of the world and King of my life!
Jesus reigns in the Heavens and on the Earth
His Kingdom will never end!

He has on his garment and on his thigh a name written, "KING OF KINGS, AND LORD OF LORDS."

Revelation 19:16 WEB

My Mighty Savior

He died on the cross and saved me from sin
He gives me life to the full, and life everlasting!

Jesus is indeed the savior of the world.

John 4:42

He is the Way, the Truth, and the Life

Jesus is the only way to the Father
Staying close to Him means
I won't lose my way!

"I am the way, the truth, and the life. No one comes to the Father, except through me".

John 14:6 WEB

A Word from the Author

Your opinion matters to me! If you enjoyed reading this book, I would greatly appreciate it if you could take a few minutes to leave a review on Amazon. Your kind feedback is appreciated and inspires me to keep doing more.
Thank you!

www.ingramcontent.com/pod-product-compliance
Lightning Source LLC
Chambersburg PA
CBHW062002130526
44582CB00045B/137